INITIAL COIN OFFERINGS (ICOS) AND START UP FUNDING

PETRU VANTU

INTRODUCTION

If you are asked what the birth of cryptocurrency would bring to the world of finance, the first thing that will probably cross your mind is what is cryptocurrency? This thought, however, will only come to the mind of people who are not well versed with the existing online currencies. But, if you are one of the few but dominant figures who know cryptocurrencies even if your eyes are closed, you would be able to answer the question more elaborately.

So to speak the actual start of the turmoil existed when bitcoin was introduced to the world and eventually became the most famous and wanted cryptocurrency. This project was started primarily to answer the lingering complains of people whose money and assets are held by one centralized unit (and often intervened by the government itself) and whose transfers are limited and frozen at a timely basis. With the start of Bitcoin, many had the option to acquire an online coin or currency that they can use similarly with fiat money. Although ac□uiring it is tedious and requires resources, many were attracted to it from the very start because many were wanting to break away with the confinement of a single entity controlling everything else in terms of finance.

Slowly, Bitcoin started to gain actual monetary value and new types of cryptocurrencies came into existence as a possible answer to the problems that Bitcoin imposes and also to create their own currencies that people can opt to use as the one generated from the former is limited and hard to acquire. Although cryptocurrency was not widely accepted, it slowly gained its momentum and now, many other businesses even accept it as a form of payment or exchange. The very same thing is slowly happening to new cryptocurrencies. Although the profits are not guaranteed and the software running them is open-source, many still try to vie to ac□uire these currencies as another means of investment.

If this kind of merge between technology and finance continues to improve over time, it will be no wonder if more and more people will divert their attention to ac□uiring these coins and more businesses will open themselves to exchanging and accepting them as actual reward or trade for good and services. Like everything else, the slow but steady approach of cryptocurrency could result in major changes in the way finance has been seen and treated in the past.

More people are opening their minds to the existence and stability of such platforms and many are craving to break away from the scrutinizing eyes of the governing bodies involved in the storage and exchange of their assets. The future may seem dim this day but as more creative minds work together to make more convenience in the way finance and everything monetary is treated.

The ICO is an revolutionary new way to get funded, and everyone wants in. The ICO, short for initial coin offering, followed several similar, e□ually successful funding events, and the numbers are rising.

Thanks again for downloading this book, I'm sure you'll enjoy reading it!

Content

CHAPTER ONE

ICO (INITIAL COIN OFFERINGS)

WHAT IS ICO?

ICO is the abbreviation of Initial Coin Offering. It means that someone offers investors some units of a new cryptocurrency or crypto-token in exchange against cryptocurrencies like Bitcoin or Ethereum. Over years now, ICOs are often used to fund the development of new cryptocurrencies. The pre-created token can be easily sold and traded on all cryptocurrency exchanges if there is demand for them.

The first token sale (also known as an ICO) was held by Mastercoin in July 2013. Ethereum raised money with a token sale in 2014, raising 3,700 BTC in its first 12 hours, e□ual to approximately $2.3 million dollars. An ICO was held by Karmacoin in April 2014 for its Karmashares project. ICOs and token sales are now extremely popular. As of May 2017, there were currently around 20 offerings a month, and a new web browser Brave's ICO generated about $35 million in under 30 seconds.

With the success of Ethereum ICO are more and more used to fund the development of a crypto project by releasing token which is somehow integrated into the project. With this turn, ICO has become a tool that could revolutionize not just currency but the whole financial system. ICO token could become the securities and shares of tomorrow.

Examples for successful Initial coin offering on Ethereum are:

- Augur
- Melonport
- Golem
- ICONOMI
- Singular DTV
- First Blood
- Digix DAO.

The legal state of ICO is mostly undefined. Ideally, the token is sold not as a financial asset but as a digital good like many other things. This is why ICO is often called "crowd sale". In this case, in the most jurisdiction, the funding with an ICO is not regulated, which makes it extremely easy and paperless, given a lawyer experienced with the issue is on board. However, some jurisdictions seem to be aware of ICO and tend to regulate them similar to the sale of shares and securities. The spectacular implosion of the DAO did a good job in kindle regulators attention. So while ICO currently mostly happen in a gray area, in the future they most likely will be regulated. This could bear some financial and legal risks for investors. Also, the cost and effort to comply with regulation could reduce the advantages of ICO compared with traditional means of funding.

HISTORY OF ICO

Let's have a look what's going on of the market for ICO. In the past years, there have been a couple of wildly successful ICO.

Hot past Cryptocurrency ICO

- **Ripple**

Ripple Labs created 100 billion XRP-token which serve as an anti-spam mechanism in the payment network Ripple, as you have to pay your network fees in XRP. The XRP are sold by Ripple Labs; their value doesn't move in a clear direction, while the trend is more downwards. It started with around 5,000 Satoshi, sometimes felt below 1,000 Satoshi, raised above 7,000 and finally fell again to a new low of 600 Satoshi, before again raising on 3,000.

- **Next**

Next was an new gen cryptocurrency made in 2013. For a start, the 1 billion token was sold to early investors. With the ICO the developers only got a double digits amount of Bitcoins. Today the NXT token, however, are worth much more and Next has become a relatively successful and stable cryptocurrency.

- **Mastercoin**

In 2013 Mastercoin announced to build an layer on top of Bitcoin and sold the Mastercoin-token to investors. The developers received around 10,000 Bitcoin, which has been worth $1mio at this time. Mastercoin token gained value some month later; some investors made huge profits. Later Mastercoin merged with Counterparty and Omni.

- **Ethereum**

The largest ICO by now was made by Ethereum. With a presale of around 60mio ETH, the Ethereum Foundation raised around 31,500 Bitcoin. This event has become one of the biggest crowdfunding ever and the start of a wildly successful cryptocurrency. The investors of the ETH-presale profited massively.

- **Lisk**

Based on BitShares, Lisk is a JavaScript written Blockchain which enables smart contracts on sidechains. Lisk sold the coins for Bitcoins and received around $5m.

- **Hot past Ethereum token ICO**

While most ICO in the past has been restricted to building an new cryptocurrency, the smart contracts of Ethereum enable startups also to use ICOs to fund development. Most of them are working with Ethereum itself and trick their presold token somehow in the process. Some examples:

- **Augur**

The decentralized prediction market uses so-called REP-token to decide on the outcome of events. 80 percent of these tokens have been sold to fund the development and got the team more than $5m. Today all the token are worth more than $100m.

- **Golem**

The Golem project aims to create a decentralized supercomputer, to which participants can contribute with their own computer and earn money by selling its power. Golem uses the Ethereum blockchain for smart contracts; the GNT token is needed to pay for the services. The ICO was restricted on 820,000,000 tokens, for which the developers received more than 10,000 BTC. Today the market share of Golem is beyond 50,000 BTC.

- **ICONOM**

Iconomi is a platform for the management of virtual assets. The ICN token is something like shares on the platform and should receive parts of the profits. The developers sold 85,000,000 token and got more than 17,000 BTC for it. Today it has a market capitalization of nearly 40,000 BTC.

- **First Blood**

The Asian platform for decentralized Sportsbet finished the ICO of its token in some seconds. Most of them have been bought by a Chinese exchange.

- **SingularDTV**

SingularDTV wants to merge Ethereum, smart contracts and the production and stream of videos. With the ICO the platform raised more than 12,000 BTC. Today the whole tokens are worth around 40,000 BTC.

SingularDTV wants to merge Ethereum, smart contracts and the production and stream of videos. With the ICO the platform raised more than 12,000 BTC. Today the whole tokens are worth around 40,000 BTC.

The token of above ICO can be bought and traded on exchanges. Some additional ICO has just finished some time ago and prepare to release the newly created token on the Ethereum Blockchain. This are the following projects:

- **Melonport**

Like Iconomi Melonport aims to develop a platform for the management of blockchain assets built upon Ethereum. The MLN token the developers sold will be needed to use the platform and have been sold or more than 2,000 BTC few month ago.

- **Qtum**

This project wants to build a platform for the easy creation and use of blockchain based smart contracts. For this mission, it could raise more than 14,000 Bitcoin in an ICO.

- **Chrono Bank**

The "uber of recruitment" intends to build a platform with its own currency for freelance projects. They sold 710,000 tokens for more than 4,000 Bitcoin.

- **Dfinity**

Similar to Golem, Dfinity wants to build a decentralized platform for cloud computing. In its ICO it raised more than 3,000 Bitcoin.

- **BlockPay With "only" about 1,000**

With "only" about 1,000 Bitcoin, the ICO of BlockPay was one of the smaller ICOs. BlockPay is a startup building a payment processor for several cryptocurrencies.

With "only" about 1,000 Bitcoin, the ICO of BlockPay was one of the smaller ICOs. BlockPay is a startup building a payment processor for several cryptocurrencies.

- **DAO Creation Period**

The DAO stands for Decentralized Autonomous Organization and it was a smart contract system built on Ethereum meant to function as a community managed venture fund. The DAO was the most successful crowdfunding project ever held as it gathered roughly $150 millions in a 28 day period.

The DAO Creation period started on May 28, 2016, and ended on the 25th of June, during this period users were allowed to purchase newly created DAO tokens with Ether (ETH).

During the first 15 days, the conversion rate for DAO tokens to ETH was 100-1, and it rose gradually by 0.05 ETH per day after until it reached the 100-1.5 scale.

Since The DAO had no owner, no one was in control of the funds meaning that during the ICO or Creation period, users sent Ether to a smart contract address that would, in turn, create DAO tokens and send them to the address from which the Ether came from.

One of the unique aspects about the DAO Initial Coin Offering was the risk-free investment option, in which a user could always recover the Ether sent on a 1-100 scale, by splitting these DAO tokens, regardless of their market price.

The DAO was hacked and the project has come to an end after an hard-fork was executed to retrieve the funds stolen. DAO holders can now withdraw ETH from the DAO on a 1-100 exchange rate.

- **Waves ICO**

The Waves Platform is a custom token and asset platform focused on business applications with features like custom token and asset issuance and exchange, fiat gateways and crowdfunding tools. The Waves Platform is currently unfinished and most of these features are still in development. The Waves ICO started on the 12th of April and lasted until the 31st of May. During the first day, users received a 20% bonus. The Waves ICO is an example of an "overbought" ICO (despite Waves being a promising project), with 29636 BTC and 460 BTC in NXT asset swaps being exchanged for Waves. The token has been trading under ICO value since the beginning of its release on exchanges, which can also be attributed to delays in the Roadmap.

- **Stratis ICO**

Stratis is a blockchain as a service (BaaS) platform that allows corporations to create their own custom private or public sidechains for their business needs. Stratis allows users to combine various features from other blockchains and to test various variations of blockchain specifications and features. The Stratis ICO took place from the 21st of July to the 26 and it gathered 915 BTC, a relatively small amount compared to other ICOs since its release Stratis has increased in value +400%. Users received a 20% bonus during the first five days, which was then reduced to 10% for the next ten days, and then 5% for the ten days.

Present ICO

- **Humaniq** (a wallet for the unbanked), aeternity ("scalable smart contracts interfacing with real-world data"), Internet of Coins (a distributed environment for several blockchains) and Cosmos (similar: "a network of distributed ledgers").

- **Blockchain Capital.** Traditional investment company which funds a lot of companies in the cryptocurrency ecosystem like BitGo, BitFury, Blockstream, BTCC, Coinbase, Ethcore, Kraken, and Ripple. With the ICO Blockchain Capital enables everybody to participate in its investment rounds.

Hot FutureICOS

Since some months the Ethereum community waits for the start of the Gnosis ICO. Like Augur Gnosis will become a decentralized prediction market on Ethereum. Since it is developed by a respected Ethereum developer stakes are high. Also, the launch of EtherEx, a decentralized cryptocurrency exchange, is eagerly awaited. While not as prominent as Gnosis, EtherEx promises to become a part of a truly decentralized ecosystem on Ethereum. Same goes for Akasha, a decentralized social network governed by the Ethereum blockchain. ICO is expected, but no date is announced by now.

With Rootstock and Hivemind, two sidechain ICO are anticipated. However, it is not known if the developers of Rootstock and Hivemind plan to presale tokens. They did not announce it, but the structure of their projects implicates tokens, and somehow these tokens have to be distributed.

HOW TO DO A SUCCESSFUL INITIAL COIN OFFERING (AND NOT GET SUED)

Typically for a successful Initial Coin Offering (for both the founders and token holders), there must be a problem where blockchain has a uni□ue value proposition to solve this problem. There should be a team in place (largely this is what you are buying at this stage) and there should be work done, and evidence of work done.

There is a vast landscape of existing legal precedent that may apply to your situation, and professional counsel tailored for your specific situation is a good idea.

Legal hurdles to overcome:

- Incorporation
- Terms and Conditions
- Securities Laws
- Commodities Laws
- Tax
- AML/KYC
- Consumer Protection

1. Incorporation

First and foremost it's suggested that any company, operating as such - setup an legal entity and declare a jurisdiction, and venture for dispute resolution. By defining these terms from the outset, you clear any ambiguity. This does not preclude you from laws applying when dealing with certain laws of customers or investors who reside or are citizen of certain countries. However, leaving it without a legal entity exposes you to be classified as a general partnership, with general liability attached to each partner, jointly and severally. This is not ideal.

Picking a friendly jurisdiction, perhaps one with a regulatory sandbox which allows you to operate within the bounds of the law is the idea scenario. Even more ideal would be if you could secure a 'non-action' letter from a specific regulator, but these are burdensome to obtain and regulators will be reluctant to completely waive liability. In order to help pick a proper jurisdiction, you might compare the laws, the details in the companies act, and the securities regulator.

2. Terms and Conditions

Laying out clear terms and conditions that define risks, uses, warranties, liability and other core and fundamental legal issues is crucial to a successful Initial Coin Offering.
Nothing should be left to chance and one should make effort for every contingency to be defined. Taking the DAO approach of "law is code!" is a dangerous and oblivious action.
The terms and conditions should be the legal communication between your project and the public, and hence the language used is of significant import- but all the communication must be taken into consideration. If your terms and conditions are watertight, but the founder is tweeting "guaranteed returns, buy your ICO today!" then this may be noticed by regulators.

- **Securities Laws**

Securities laws are complex and vary from jurisdiction to jurisdiction. However, the quick summary is that you generally would NOT want to be regulated as a security. {Unless your asset is, in fact, a security, and you want to be treated as such). This would re□uire registration in the United States with the SEC.
The first thing to examine in a transaction is the motivation behind a token. Is the buyer's primary motivation for buying the token that of investment or anticipated future profit? This is likely to be a security.

- Is this buyer interested in a minor asset, consumer good, or participation which helps the seller with early cash flow difficulties, or to advance a consumer purpose - this is obviously less likely to be construed by either the consumer or courts as a 'security'.
- What is the plan of distribution? Is there common trading for speculation or investment.
- Thirdly, look to see what the reasonable expectations of the investing public would be.

Finally - is there an existing regulatory scheme where the token sale can take shelter? This may reduce the risk of the instrument.

1. Commodities laws

In jurisdictions where the asset being traded or sold - sometimes there can be a regulator who regulates commodities separately. In the United States, this would be the CFTC.

If your coin represents an underlying asset- then that asset may be regulated. For instance, if your coin is representing gold - which is a commodity, then it may fall under purview of a commodities regulator.

2. AML/KYC

One of the most difficult areas for a crowdsale owner to participate is the AML/KYC laws. If you are distributing coins to known terrorists or members who are on a watchlist (think OFAC, etc.) then you may be committing a crime. In the US this would fall under the jurisdiction of the Office of foreign assets and control, under the treasury department, who administers and enforces economic and trade sanctions. There are certain jurisdictions which make KYC/AML easier to comply with than other jurisdictions.

Essentially know your customer laws re□uire that owners of a company be identified by their government-issued documents - absent of which, you may be considered to be aiding and abetting economic terrorism. If you don't know their name, (or if they are a terrorist), then how could you be expected to perform sanctions screening? The law has an answer to this □uestion, that you are still responsible to find out their name.

How Much KYC Should You Collect?

If your company is a regulated entity, then there are laws or regulations prescribing the amount of KYC to collect (for instance, government-issued ID + a utility bill for a natural person). However, it is likely your entity may be considered non-regulated, in which case collecting KYC only needs to satisfy the minimum re□uired by that jurisdiction. Again, this is complex as you may not be operating in any specific jurisdiction, which opens you up generally to any jurisdiction where they have residents who are investing or participating in your ICO.

Do You Really Need To Collect KYC?

As cryptotokens are a new invention, laws have not caught up to the pace at which technology moves. Because of this - it's a bit of a grey area whether KYC needs to be collected for an ICO or not. If you consider your ICO a security - then yes - absolutely KYC needs to be collected and also you need to determine whether the purchaser is a accredited or professional investor. However, if you consider your ICO as a token for use in your product - then typically there isn't an re□uirement for you to check each and every customer. This could, however, be disputed, as while in daily commerce not every transaction is screened against sanctions lists - businesses are not allowed (or not legally allowed) to do business with someone who is on a sanctions list.

DIFFERENT BETWEEN ICOS AND IPOS

ICOs have been compared to Initial Public Offerings (IPOs) of corporations. There are some notable similarities - both of them are used to sell a stake and raise money, and both have investors who see the potential and risk their capital in order to make a potential profit.

However, there are significant differences as well. ICOs are mostly supported by early enthusiasts and not professional investors. In that respect, they are similar to 'kickstarter campaigns', but with the backers having a financial stake in the project. ICOs are also not regulated or registered with any government organization and there are usually no investor protections other than what is built into the platform itself.

Most ICOs today are marketed as 'software presale tokens' akin to giving early access to a online game to early supporters. In order to try to avoid legal re□uirements that come with any form of a security sale, many ICOs today use language such as 'crowdsale' or 'donation' instead of ICOs. They also use legal disclaimers and language to the participants that this isn't a securities sale. It is unclear whether this is sufficient for global jurisdictions to treat it differently from a securities sale. To date, the matter hasn't been litigated in a court of law.

EVALUATING INITIAL COIN OFFERING (ICO) INVESTMENTS

Many factors influence the chances for a successful ICO and they can predict whether it will be valuable for its investors. Note: ICOs are a high-risk way of fundraising. Never invest anything you can't completely afford to lose. Keep in mind that due to a lack of regulation, you will have difficulty getting back your lost money in case of any failures.

1. Team Composition

Find out everything you can about the team, especially the development team and the advisory board. Look up each team member for relevant experience. Google their names. Visit their LinkedIn profiles. Look for famous names among the advisory board of the project. Find out if the team has any crypto experience and more importantly - in which projects, or ICOs, they were involved with and the impact they had.

2. Bitcointalk.org Thread

A good starting point is the project's announcement (ANN) thread on BitcoinTalk.org, as Bitcointalk is the biggest forum for Bitcoin and crypto related issues. It is strongly recommended that you read the messages carefully. Investor's concerns will be answered (or maybe unanswered) in this thread. It is a bad sign when the developers avoid answering certain questions or aren't collaborating. Sending devs a personal message to see how responsive they are is also a good idea.

Each message on Bitcointalk contains the rank and activity degree (number of past messages) of the sender. Be aware of newbies and low-ranking writers. Reputation has become very important and significant.

Be aware of experienced writerscomments and also look for negative messages, sometimes it could be a warning sign. Use Select [All] to see all comments in the thread and use CTRL + F (Windows) to search for red flag words like 'scam', 'con', 'MLM'. See the relation between the search results and the total number of replies.

3. Stage Of The Project And VC Investments

Evaluate the stage of the project. Does it only have a whitepaper? A beta version? Is there a launched product with limited functionality? Prefer projects which have "some lines" of working code, however, many ICOs have proven they can become success stories without any code written.

VCs (venture capital) tend to invest and support projects from early stages. Look for this information usually on the main page of the project's website. It's likely to be considerable if a well-known crypto VC is involved, like Blockchain Capital or Fenbushi (belongs to Vitalik Buterin - founder of Ethereum).

4. Community AndMedi

It is crucial to have a wide open supporting community like a public Slack for all investors. Openness is as crucial in gaining our trust as the Github code. Try to grasp the atmosphere within the community. Look at the size of the community and its activity.

5. What Do They Need The Token For? Is The Blockchain Necessary?

ICOs mean the creation of a newly dedicated token for the project. One of the most important questions each project needs to answer is what is the token for? Why isn't Bitcoin or Ethereum enough to serve as the project's token? Yes, many projects just make up a scammy story. Hey, an ICO can't be an ICO without a dedicated token. The same □uestion needs to be asked regarding the use of the blockchain technology behind the project.

6. Unlimited / Hard Cap

In the early days of crypto ICOs, the difference between open and hard cap didn't have the same impact as today's ICOs. An open cap allows investors to send unlimited funding to the project's ICO wallet. The more coins are circulating, the less uni□ue your tokens become for the trading afterward - through less demand.

As ICOs become mainstream within the crypto land, enormous amounts are collected. Take a look at Bancor, this project raised an astonishing $150 million in just three hours. This resulted in no percentage gain for the investors. Keep that in mind when participating in ICOs with no cap.

On the other hand, you don't want to be the only one investing in the project. Exchange's have much less interest in projects that raise very little, which makes it harder to sell these tokens after release.

7. Token Distribution - When And How

Greed can be defined by a high token distribution to the team members, let's say, more than 50% of the tokens is suspicious. A good project will link its token distribution to the roadmap. Because each phase or milestone of the project requires a certain amount of funding.

Watch for the token distribution stage. Some projects just release their tokens hours after the ICO has ended. Some projects need to develop a beta version before sending out the tokens. If you look at the percentage gain of Etherium (one year between ICO and token distribution, around 500% gain), Augur (1+ years, 1500%) and Decent (8 months, 350%), sometimes this break creates a very positive hype around the project.

8. Evaluating The Whitepaper

Most typical investors actually don't read through the whitepaper, even though it contains all the necessary information about the upcoming project and the ICO.

Don't hesitate to read it, or at least the majority of it. Note the strong and negative aspects and add in some of your own research. In the end, the whitepaper is the silver platter to potential investors. After reading it you should be able to answer a simple question - what kind of value does this project bring to our world? You'll also learn what you're investing in.

9. Quality Of The Code - Meet Githhub

If you have a little bit of programming experience, you should be using it here. The quality of a developer can be understood by analyzing some of their code. As a non-techie, it is still possible to evaluate their □uality by looking at the consistency of the code. Another good indicator is the usage of proper commenting. Avoid messy developers. A piece of code reflects the attitude of a developer.

Next, the length of a function is another indicator. A function containing more than 50 lines of code should raise a red flag. Modularity is important and makes the code more readable and maintainable.

10. The Bottom Line

ICOs will become more and more 'mainstream' as a method for raising funds. There will be plenty of projects to choose from, hence it will become even harder to assess these projects.

It is key to investigate and read as much information as possible and write down all the important aspects, positive and negative, before making an investment decision.

HOW TO BUY DURING AN ICO

1. Get Bitcoin Or Ether.
This is easily done at leading cryptocurrency exchange and wallet Coinbase. Hook up your bank account or credit card, make a purchase, and then wait a few days for your bank to process it. Just make sure to do it at least a week in advance of the token sale you want to participate in, as it takes days for these transactions to go through since they use the traditional banking system. Also note that on Coinbase, the fee for using credit cards is higher 3.99%, as opposed to 1.49% for bank transactions.
If you plan to keep some bitcoin or ether here, move the bitcoin into the vault, and make sure not to use two-factor authentication via SMS but instead on Google Authenticator or a Yubikey.
2. Move Your Bitcoin Or Ether To A Wallet You Control.
This step is important because you cannot participate in an ICO from your Coinbase account. The reason for this is that when you use a centralized service such as a company like Coinbase, you do not own the private keys to your bitcoin or ether address. The way the ICOs typically work, you send them your ether or bitcoin, and the smart contract immediately sends the tokens back to your address. But since you don't have private keys in a Coinbase account, if you send ether or bitcoin to an ICO address from your Coinbase account, you'll simply be enriching Coinbase instead of getting your desired tokens.

If you're using ether, which is commonly accepted in ICOs, you can use a site like My Ether Wallet to create a new Ethereum key there and transfer your ethers on Coinbase to that wallet. Another option is Parity, which enables you to do things like invest in an ICO at an exact time – a feature that you might want to use if you believe the ICO will sell out within seconds. If you're using Bitcoin, Blockchain.info has a good user-controlled wallet. (Many token sales accept other coins as well, but bitcoin and ether are the two most popular.) Once you've transferred your coins to a user-controlled wallet, you'll have an ether or bitcoin address whose private key you control – and that means that you'll be able to receive tokens there as well.

3. Participate In The ICO By Sending Your Crypto To Their Address.

The token sale will post an address where money is being collected during a certain window of time. Be very careful that the address to which you are sending coins is actually the address of the token sale. Scams trying to get people to send their ether and bitcoin elsewhere abound. In fact, yesterday, during its ICO, Coindash.io's website got hacked, and the crooks appear to have made off with $7.9 million worth of ether simply by changing the address on the website to their own.

It's also possible to use a smart contract to make your bid. During the crowdsale for prediction market Gnosis, which I wrote about in the July cover story, because there was concern the crowdsale would be over □uickly, people who were, say, living in a part of the world where they'd likely be asleep during the ICO made their bids via smart-contract-powered bidding rings. Because of the time crunch that occurs during many ICOs, many investors try to get in before others during a limited window by paying exorbitant fees to make sure their transaction goes through □uickly. For the Gnosis ICO, these bidding rings collected people's money beforehand and made the bid for them at the appropriate time, thereby saving individual investors money because the exorbitant fee was now split all bidding ring participants, rather than just one person shouldering it. This also meant that the investors didn't need to trust a person or institution to return their fair share of tokens to them.

4. Once You Have Your Tokens, Figure Out How To Store Them.

If you have a significant amount of money invested, it's best to use a cold wallet (one not connected to the internet), and particularly a hardware wallet, which is a device specifically designed to hold bitcoin, ether, and other crypto tokens securely. The two most popular hardware wallets are Trezor and Ledger. Whichever you get, plug it into a USB port, transfer your coins to the address that comes with your hardware wallet, and afterward, unplug it from your computer. You've just stored your coins so they are secure even from viruses on your computer.

If you lose your hardware wallet, you can re-create it using what's called a paper backup — a series of words that you can use to obtain your private keys again.

5. If You Want To Store A Coin Not Supported By Your Hardware Wallet ...

This isn't very common now that almost all tokens follow what's called the ERC-20 standard (a standardized token on the Ethereum network), but in case you have an obscure coin that isn't supported, one option is to store those coins in an encrypted text file on a USB drive. Afterward, unplug it from your computer and keep it stored in a safe place such as a safety deposit box until you need to use the coins.
Again, create a piece of paper with the information necessary to re-create the private keys. Each coin should have a guide on how to do this since the method differs slightly coin to coin.
Another option would be to store those coins on an exchange. However, if you do so, be sure to secure those coins with what's called two-factor authentication, not with your phone number, but with either Google Authenticator or a Yubikey.

HOW TO BUY TOKENS AFTER THEIR ICO

1. Get bitcoin or ether.
2. Transfer it to an exchange that has the coins you want to buy.
Typically, crypto exchanges Poloniex, Kraken or Bittrex have a large number of tokens on offer, including some of the newest ones.
When you find an exchange offering the token you want, create an account and obtain your address on that exchange. Copy it, and then go to Coinbase and paste that address into the send box. Within a few minutes, your money will show up on that exchange.
3. Set Up Two-Factor Authentication On Your Account, But Not With Your Phone Number.

This is an incredibly important step, and the part about not doing this with your phone number is key. Do not skip this step and do not use your phone number for security unless you are willing to let hackers come and steal your coins, which they will do.

They have been targeting people both well-known and not well-known in the crypto space and plundering their accounts on centralized exchanges. Their method is to persuade a customer service rep at a telco that they are their target (say, you) and that "you" want to move the money from, say, Sprint to T-Mobile (in reality, their device). Once all the phone numbers and cell phone messages meant for you are going to their phone, they then go to your crypto and other accounts (such as your Kraken or bank account or Gmail or Twitter or Dropbox) and select "forgot password." If you have two-factor via SMS or text message enabled, they now change your password, lock you out and move your bitcoin or ether to their own wallet – and since crypto transfers are not reversible, you will then be out of luck.

Instead of using your phone number for backup, use the Google Authenticator app, which creates new codes tied to each specific service at short intervals, or an external device such as the Yubikey.

1. Exchange Your BTC OrETH For The Token.

Once your tokens on a centralized wallet are safe from being whisked away by two-factor via SMS, find the trading pair you want. Let's say you have bitcoins and want to exchange them for REP, the coin of the prediction market Augur, which launches this August. Choose how many tokens you want to buy, and if you're making a limit order, how much bitcoin you'd like to pay per REP.

1. Store Them Securely In A Hardware Wallet.

If you're not planning to trade, transfer your new coins to your own hardware wallet as outlined above. Then, be sure to secure that, perhaps putting it into a safety deposit box at a bank and keeping your recovery backup in more than one geographically distinct and secure locations.

CHAPTER TWO

START UP FUNDING

INTRODUCTION TO STARTUP FUNDING

For any type of business, be it big, small or home-based, startup funding is a mandatory aspect of the business plan and is definitely the stepping stone to success. You will be surprised to learn that most of the multi-millionaires and billionaires of today just started with great ideas and very fewer funds. Monetary backing is an essential aspect of every business and although the situation does get complicated at times, it is definitely a necessity and an inevitable part of your business as well.

In today's business world, the only bridge between success and failure is the way you make your decisions.

FIVE REASONS BUSINESS START-UP FUNDING IS ESSENTIAL

1. For preserving your capital: Before starting your business, you must have to save sufficient amount of money for your business but over the period of time, you might run into unexpected obstacles. This is the reason why you must secure business startup funding so that you can comfortably cover the initial cost of your business and you can also save enough money which can cover the unexpected expenses.
2. For building a strong foundation: Every business is like a building and re□uires a strong foundation so that it can be successful in its venture and laying the strong foundation is necessary to have adequate funding. You should avoid taking the generating income from shaky groundwork and your startup funding will help you in this by helping you to pay the bills until the first checks start pouring in.
3. Helping you to beat the odds: You will be surprised to learn that more than 25% of the American businesses fail in their first year itself which is mainly because of the lack of funds. Ade□uate funding is a must to ensure that your business continues without any obstacles. Searching the right startup funding becomes mandatory in this case as this will help you to prevent your business boat from rocky surfaces.
4. Supporting faster expansion: A consistent flow of cash is a must in order to meet the needs and demands of the customers. If you have a solid base of business, then it will definitely help you in building your reserves.
5. For enhancing your reputation: No one wants to do business with a company that is struggling to keep their stance in the market. If you want to create a good business reputation for yourself, then the startup funds is the right answer to this situation.

START-UPS AND FINANCING ERRORS

It is a fact that more and more people are taking the risk of becoming self-employed and exploring their dream of setting up their own business. This growing trend has left business start-up funds an ever-growing commodity.

Most small business start-ups fail within the first 5 years and a lot of the reasons for this come down to the way in which they attempt to generate finance for their businesses. In order to ensure the longevity of your business, you need to avoid the errors involved in looking for financial support.

One of the biggest mistakes you can make when trying to generate finance for your business startup is by going to 1 lender for 100% of your business finance. Also don't go to a lender looking for 100% of your startup capital, if you can look to use between 20 - 30% of your own personal funds.

Before your going to have a chance at getting your hands on any money, you are going to need a solid business plan stating exactly where that money is going. It also helps the lender to catch the vision of what your company is, where it is going and why they should assist you to make it a reality.

Another huge mistake that can be seen in 80% of business plans is under projecting spending. Don't think for one second that you have more chance of winning a lender over if your costs are less, even if you do get the funds it won't be enough leaving everyone involved in a difficult situation.

Do you have a marketing plan? If not this needs to be done before you start asking for an investor to finance your business. How much is the marketing going to cost, is it going to provide a good ROI, are you going to be able to reach your target audience. These are all □uestions you should have taken into consideration long before your meeting with the bank.

THREEMAJOR SOURCESOF FUNDING STARTUPS

- **Bootstrapping**

The best way to build a company is without the help of any financer. And it is possible also. Bootstrapping basically means building a company with the blend some of personal savings and borrowed cash from family and friends. Some of the clever founders get back a huge amount of their money by starting their company in countries where the living cost is comparatively low like Chile or Vietnam. Also, with the help of government grants, they are able to grow easily until the returns start rolling in. A few crowdfunding platforms encourage cash donations from the public in exchange for early access to company's products. This has made it easier for the founders to get capital without giving up a valuable e□uity.

- **Equity Funding**

If bootstrapping is not a likely option for the founders, then they can craft a stake in the company for investment purpose. Whereas risking wealthy firms are best for startups that re□uire lot of cash and aim to grow □uickly. Not to forget there are □uite a lot of other e□uity options for organizers with diverse business ideas. New founders must try and get their company into an accelerator. They have a two-three month program which is basically designed to aid new startups to work through the initial phases of the development. This program also helps you to find possible investors at the end of the program. Accelerators have also launched a few success stories, whose organizers have received some funding and valuable guidance from some of the skilled entrepreneurs in return for a 7% to 10% stake in their businesses.

- **Debt Funding**

It is not advisable for a young startup to go to debt funding in its early stage. It must be something of a last option. But in some cases, a small amount of cash is re□uired at the earliest. In these cases, it makes sense for the company to take out steady, old loan and spare the trouble of finding an investor. In such cases, it is advisable to check if the business is eligible for any government-aided loans. Such loans usually have promising rate of interests and malleable repayment plans.

BEST WAYS TO REDUCESTART-UP FUNDING FOR NEW BUSINESS

First of all, you should get advice from a certified small business start-up efficiency professional. This person can help guide you in the development of a solid business start-up funding plan.

In order to be successful and lower business start-up funding, you need to choose your industry wisely. Don't rush into a business in which you have little or no experience. This lack of knowledge and experience can lead to underestimating how much business start-up funding you'll need to keep your business alive - this could mean disaster for your new business.

Below are proven techniques for new business entrepreneurs to reduce costs, increase sales and have a healthier profit margin:

• **The Call is Free!** When your company has a toll-free phone number, it encourages not only local, but out-of-state customers to give you a ring to find out more about your business. The cost of a toll-free number is low, low, low.

• **Just the Fax!** Subscribe to an e-fax service and get faxes sent to your e-mailbox as a PDF document.

• **Image is everything!** Get your company Logo created and start branding your company - put the logo on everything - business cards, stationary, flyers, website - even T-shirts and coffee mugs!

• **Don't Weave a Tangled Web**. Create a website with a search-engine friendly format. Low-cost hosting combined with free Word Press templates make it easy to promote and build your company image. The Word Press blog websites deliver visibility n Bing, Google and Yahoo searches.

• **Go Government!** There are two government agencies that provide help to small business owners: The Small Business Administration (SBA) and the Department of Defense (DoD). The SBA offers local and regional support such as counseling programs, briefings with prime contractors and government agencies, small business loans and free government bid matching services.

• **Hire Interns!** Many local high schools, community colleges and universities place interns in local accounting, entrepreneurship, internet and marking businesses. They work for free to gain experience - and you'll gain a dedicated and ambitious employee!

• **Bring Retirees Back!** You can find highly experienced managers to serve as board members, advisory board members or voluntary staff members. They have years of experience and - best of all - connections!

A SIMPLE PLAN FOR BUSINESS START-UPFUNDING WITHOUT CREATING DEBT

1. Covering Start-Up Costs

Ideally, your introduction to the small business world lies in starting out slowly. Rather than quitting your job, obtaining business start-up funding and sinking all of your faith into your new venture, start by operating your business on the side of your day job. Cut down to part-time hours if possible, but make sure you have a solid, regular income to support you during the early stages.

Your next step is to then investigate exactly how much it will cost you to get started.

Depending on your business idea, basic start-up expenses can include licenses and registration costs, banking fees, legal consultations, stationary and office expenses, accountant fees and insurance. If you start small, you can avoid spending more than a few hundred dollars on these items.

The important thing is that you're able to trade, so at the top of the priority list is get the correct licenses and business registrations in place.

Setting up correct accounting procedures won't matter until you're making money, so don't spend any money here until you have to. Instead, create a simple excel spreadsheet to monitor your costs and income in the beginning stages, and then use your first month's profits to pay for an accountant to professionally set up your books.

Also, if you're trading online, direct your customers to pay via PayPal. You'll pay a percentage of incoming payments in fees to PayPal, but you can avoid having to fork over for an expensive business banking account.

A few other cost-saving techni□ues include:

- **Take The Pressure Off.** If you don't need too much space, work from home in the beginning. Why spend $300 a week to rent an office if you don't have to?
- **DIY Your Business Cards And Letterheads.** There are countless free templates available online, and you can print them yourself for literal pennies.
- **Don't Over Indulge.**Only buy the office equipment and stationary that you really need, rather than the things that you want. Stapler and pens? Definitely. Shredder and laminator? Not yet.
- **Research For The Best Price.**Before you buy anything, shop around for the best prices both online and offline.
- **Get Involved Online.**For most businesses, you'll also need to consider virtual business expenses and possibly small business start-up loans. Setting up a website can cost anything from a couple of hundred dollars to tens of thousands, and you need to register your domain name/s and cover ongoing web hosting costs.

This doesn't have to cost the earth, however, particularly if you begin with a blog. Blogs can be established and hosted for free on popular sites such as wordpress.com and blogger.com, so your net outlay is simply your time. As a bonus, you can hook up Google AdSense on your blog, so as you build more traffic, you'll make money from click-through on the advertisements.

As more people begin to enjoy the benefits of shopping online, it's more important than ever that you establish an honest and reliable online presence. This is because you're essentially trying to persuade complete strangers to make a purchase from you and to do that, they need to trust you.

Positive feedback scores on eBay build trust. Genuine testimonials build trust. Even including your full name or a photo of you somewhere on your website will encourage people to trust you, as you will be seen to be standing by your product.

All of the above will help to solidify your online footprint and build your profile as an honest and trustworthy trader. You should aim to join as may online communities and social networking websites as possible, and actively participate to establish yourself as an expert in your field, whatever that may be.

If you're launching a gardening business, for example, contribute to related forums, comment on similar blogs, and invite gardening questions on your own site. Make sure you leave your blog address as your online footprint when you sign off, and continue to nurture the valuable contacts you build along the way. Getting involved online costs very little in upfront cash, but requires a solid commitment of your time and energy.

• **Ask For More Business.**Asking for referrals is an often-overlooked method of generating sales, and there's truly no better way to save marketing and advertising dollars than by using word-of-mouth.

When you have a satisfied customer, no matter how large or small the transaction, ask for a testimonial. Most people can spare 30 seconds to reply to a brief email, so at the conclusion of your transaction, send your customers a short email with 2-3 succinct questions about their experience with you and your business.

Offer them a small discount for their return business as a reward for filling out your short survey, and ask if they know anyone else who might need your product or service. You could even offer a 'friends and family discount' to encourage their contacts to try your services. If you simply ask for the business, you'll be surprised at the response you receive.

CROWD-FUNDING - THE IDEAL WAY TO FINANCE YOUR BUSINESS

Ever heard of crowd-funding? Maybe you've seen it as "crowdfunding." Either way, not many people know what it is...or how it can help them fund their start-up or existing business. Crowd-funding is a term that's been around only a couple of years. It first became known, though only in a limited way, because of a website called Kickstarter. The current buzz, however, stems from the Jumpstart Our Business Startups Act (JOBS) signed into law by President Obama on April 5, 2012. That law allows people of means to invest in small and start-up companies, a novel but interesting option for owner's of such companies.

The Securities Exchange Commission has until roughly the end of 2012 to establish specific rules to ensure such funding will be available. Why involve the SEC? Because the people who will be investing in what will be higher-risk funding expect some protection. Regardless of what those rules turn out to be, if you intend to successfully participate in the rush for crowd-funding dollars, there is one thing you'll want to prepare in advance.

Crowd-funding isn't going to be the answer for every type of business. The most money - the smart money - is will likely fund high-tech businesses or those that best satisfy a major consumer need or want. And that funding is virtually certain to go first to companies that have a well polished, written business plan.

Yes, a written business plan, the curse of so many owners of small businesses. With crowd-funding, a well-written business plan will be a must. No one smart enough to have amassed enough money to invest in a business will be foolish enough to buy into a company that lacks a well-written business plan.

Your business plan will have to describe your company in simple terms but in terms capable of exciting a number of potential investors. What should that plan include? Much will depend on the type of business you're running or hope to start.

A typical business plan includes at least the following sub-plans: a marketing plan, a finance plan, and a sales plan. The bigger the company the more sub-plans your business plan is likely to include: an e□uipment plan, a facilities plan, an inventory plan, perhaps even a transportation plan. Those crowd-funders will also want to see financial projection - sales, profit margins, manufacturing and labor costs...at least three years of those projections.

Here are a list of the best crowdfunding platforms to look to if you are a startup entrepreneur.

1. Kickstarter: Kickstarter is probably the oldest and the strongest crowdfunding platform. With over 74k Projects launched on its website and 383M $ raised through the website for projects, Kickstarter has a success rate of 44%. It can help fund everything from films, games, and music to art, design, and technology. Kickstarter is full of ambitious, innovative, and imaginative projects that are brought to life through the direct support of others.

2. WeFunder: Wefunder is a crowd investing platform for startups. They help seed investors purchase stock for as little as $100 in the most promising new businesses around the country. They also help founders raise funds from their most passionate users who provide product feedback, marketing evangelism, and business connections. The company was founded in January 2010 by an MIT Sloan School of Management. Right now it boasts of a huge number of investments, as written on their website: 9,287 funders pledge to invest $25,989,550 in startups

3. Indigogo: Indiegogo is one of the world's largest and earliest crowdfunding websites. They have helped to raise millions of dollars for over 30,000 campaigns, across 194 countries. Danae, Eric, and Slava each tried to raise money for something they were passionate about, but they came up short. They had great ideas, the passion to work hard, and good networks, yet access to funding through traditional channels proved limited. The trio was determined to find a solution to the problem. Indiegogo was born; the crowdfunding solution that empowers ideas and enables people to donate funds easily.

4. CrowdFunder: Based in Los Angeles, crowdfunding is a social network for entrepreneurs and investors to connect, crowdfund and grow. The company puts tools, connections, and advice in the hands of business owners and investors at all stages in the life cycle of a business. Startups and small businesses can raise funds through e□uity, debt and contribution-based instruments. Crowdfunder is also holding a series of contests in cities around the US where local businesses compete, and get a chance to win funding up to US $500,000. This website however mainly concentrates on the US market.

5. RocketHub: RocketHub is a crowdfunding platform for creative professionals. There are project topics tagged with various tag words from beautiful to weird on this site. Rockethub is gaining a lot of popularity in recent times due to its continuous media exposure.

6. SeedInvest: Concentrating on American startups, this website was started by a group of MBA professionals from The Wharton School of the University of Pennsylvania, SeedInvest seamlessly brings together entrepreneurs and investors through an e□uity-based crowdfunding platform in a way that has never been done before. SeedInvest empowers entrepreneurs with a platform to pitch to millions of investors throughout the US in order to raise seed capital

7. Quirky: Quirky is a Crowdfunding Website for Inventors. According to the website, it has developed 241 products, has 188 retail partners and has a community of over 283,000 people. For centuries, becoming an "inventor" has been a hard gig to crack. Complexities relating to financing, engineering, distribution, and legalities have stood in the way of brilliant people executing on their great ideas. Since launching in 2009, Quirky has rapidly changed the way the world thinks about product development

8. Startsomegood: Startsomegood is a Crowdfunding Website for Social Entrepreneurs. Start Some Good is a new crowdfunding website for social initiatives to raise funds through a community of supporters. You can even see a project from India on this website.

9. Fundable: Founded by serial entrepreneur Wil Schroter, Fundable investors have the opportunity to invest in small business for e□uity. The website is currently running a rewards-based funding platform.

10. Believers Fund: This website is for mobile apps. This innovative crowdFunding platform has partnered with companies like Microsoft Bizspark and has oflate, become the talk of the crowdfunding niche.

STARTUP FUNDING PROPER BUDGETING

Calculating Start-Up Cost

You have a good business idea in mind and now, you have decided to turn it into a working entity.

Here is the list of start-up costs that you must be ready to spend on:

- Securing a property is the first requirement if you are not into a home-based business. You may consider buying or taking the property on lease. Security deposits for the property on lease are among the main start-up costs.
- To convert the property into a business facility, you would need to buy furniture and lighting equipment. Renovations and repairs must also be included in the cost.
- Even before you start the production of your business products, you need to invest in the research and development of the same. Even if you put up a store to sell branded products, you need to invest in market research to learn about the individual interests of people.
- Business start-up advertising and promotion to contribute toward start-up costs. Apart from offline advertising, you are re□uired to consider the cost of building website and other online promotional activities.
- At the very start of the business, you will be re□uired to buy business e□uipment and building inventory.

Business incorporation requires other costs to be taken into account. These include costs for obtaining business permit and license and fees for professionals like accountants, consultants, and attorneys.

Fixed Expenses for the First Year

Once your business is in operation, the first year will give you an idea about your fixed and variable expenses. Here are some of the fixed expenses you will bear annually:

- If you have borrowed a business loan, you need to repay the same.

• Business insurance costs are other major fixed expenses that you must take into account.
• Another major contributor toward fixed business cost is the rent you will be paying monthly. This includes rent for the property, as well as for the equipment you take on lease.
• Utility bills are other monthly expenses that a business bears in the form of fixed expenses. Phone and electricity bills are based on your usage, but they almost remain the same for each month. Internet connection bills too must be included in this category.
• Employee compensation is one significant business cost that you will be paying every month. However, this business expense may increase depending on the employees you keep hiring in the subsequent months. Similar business cost is related to the fees you pay to the accountants and business consultants

Variable Costs for First Year

There are some business expenses that keep varying from month to month or from year to year. However, you should have an idea of these expenses at the very beginning of the business so that the complete business budget can be defined accordingly.
Here are some of the most probable variable business expenses:
• Cost of buying new e□uipment and replacing the old faulty ones is variable in nature. You may spend on them for one month, or may not for the next.
• Business advertising costs is variable in nature, as you might extensively promote your business in one month or change the advertising fre□uency for the next month.

•Cost of buying raw materials and maintaining inventory also depends on the level of demand and supply in the market.

•Packaging costs, shipping costs, and business mailing costs are other expenses that are decided on a monthly basis.

•Employee commissions too depend on the monthly performance of your staff and sales executives.

Therefore, these are deemed variable business costs.

Business taxes also depend on your □uarterly and annual expenses and earnings and are variable costs. Now, the □uestion is how to prepare your budget to include all these items.

First of all, it is important to take the help of an accountant who will assist you to arrange instantly for the start-up costs and also maintain savings and funds to handle the fixed and variable costs per month.

HOW TOMAINTAIN A STEADY CASH FLOW

For any business to be successful the most important factor is the availability of ready cash and maintenance of a healthy cash flow. However, during day-to-day operation of business it is often found to be the most difficult task and every year a big percentage of the small businesses close down for lack of ready cash. Here are some tips that are really effective for small businesses to maintain a steady cash flow.

1. Incentivize Payment: If you are into one of those businesses where the clients tend to defer payments, try to introduce an incentive scheme for immediate payments. If customers would pay at the time of purchase you would not need to worry about collecting receivables and the cash flow will also be maintained at its best.

2. Credit from Vendors: Try to negotiate terms with your vendors and suppliers to get an extended credit period so that you don't need to pay promptly for your purchases. This will delay the outflow of cash from your accounts and less money will be trapped in your inventory. There are suppliers who would even offer a 60-day credit period and with such an extended period to pay you will hopefully have your receivables collected from your customers and use that to pay the vendors. This way you will not have to shell out your own cash or spend very little yet maintain proper supply of your raw materials.

3. Account Receivable Factoring: Factoring of accounts receivables is a very popular and effective way to maintain a healthy cash flow. Businesses that have long gestation period before the receivables could be converted to cash can always factor their receivables to get ready cash as per their requirements. It is particularly easy to factor your invoices if you are dealing with big companies or government agencies because the factors are more willing to take risk with invoices due from large corporations than with small businesses.

4. Ask for Advance: If you are in a business where you provide custom-made goods to your customers as per their orders you can always ask them for an advance at the time of starting the project. This would reduce the risk of nonpayment as a part of the payment is already realized. Also, a healthy cash flow can be maintained very easily if you can negotiate a term of periodic payment with the customer, so that the customer pays you in parts as you progress with the project.

5. Savings Fund: Most businesses go through seasonal changes in sales volume, sometimes its good and sometimes it is slow. It is a very good practice to keep away a certain percentage of the total revenue in the savings fund that helps to operate and run the business smoothly during hard times.

NETWORKING TO IMPROVE FUNDING EFFORTS

One of the big challenges a startup faces is getting investors to look at their company. While inventing something that's better, faster, and cheaper than anything on the market or something that is not on the market at all yet is important, investors are looking for much more than a great idea. Here are a few ways that networking can help you put your best foot forward.

1. Check out the competition - Networking groups, whether they're online where you can lurk and learn without being seen or face to face where you can engage in conversation with your competition, provide an opportunity for you to polish your pitch. Ideas that might seem brilliant in your own space can fade significantly when you have a chance to hear what others are saying and see how their messages are being received. Even if you're not in the same industry space, you're competing for carefully guarded investment funds. Investors want a message that resonates with them.

2. Observe other's pitches - A Networking group that does a regular audition for startups seeking funding with real investors sitting on the panel of judges can be a real eye-opener. The feedback that the judges offer to each of the teams auditioning their pitch for investors will be rich in content that will help you. While you're watching each hopeful team, you might start with the idea that they have it all together and end with a head full of ideas on what you need to put together for your own startup. Even the most polished looking presentation will get suggestions.

3. Build your team - One of the big mistakes startups make is in thinking that they can get funding with just the inventors and their idea. Investors are looking for a whole team. Investors are looking for a whole team with success stories behind them. They want to see that you have either engaged people for every aspect of a successful operation or, at least, know where you have a gap and are actively looking for an experienced professional with a successful track record to fill the gap. You can meet the people you need to fill out your team by networking.

Networking will help you see what is and is not working. It will provide you with opportunities to meet the right kind of people, and help you understand how to provide, clear, concise communication of your value to others. It may even bring you face to face with investors who hear and understand the value of your offering.

CONCLUSION

As a start-up, we only wish there was a green light indicator to notify you that you have reached the growth stage. The difficulty about the transition is there is no formula or indicator that sends you a rescue flare. During the start-up period, the biggest challenge an entrepreneur faces is managing their finances and continuing the flow of production. The growth stage is when your business has been around for a few years and the customers are increasing and you need to hire employees. The most critical stage of the transition is surviving the valley of death. In order to survive the valley death curve, you will need to know how to prepare for it.

According to investopedia.com, "The name "death valley" refers to the high probability that a start-up firm will die off before a steady stream of revenues is established. After a firm receives its first round of financing, it incurs a lot of initial costs. Offices are usually built, staff is hired and operating costs are incurred; meanwhile, the firm is not earning significant income. Unless a firm can effectively manage itself through the Death Valley curve, it will fall victim to negative cash flows."

The valley of death in a start-up world has two different customers, the early adopters, and the laggards. In the beginning, the first wave of people are the individuals who love your product or services. The gap between those two stages is the most crucial piece of the company growth. The growth phase is when your product or service has been validated and it's something the market wants. When your business enters into that transition you need to identify how you are going to channel it and how are you going to support the demand.

Martin Zwilling a contributor for Forbes.com says, "In order to survive the valley of death, the following 10 tips will help you:"

1. Accumulate some resources before you start.
2. Keep your day job until revenue starts to flow
3. Solicit funds from friend's and family
4. Use crowdfunding
5. Apply for contests and business grants
6. Get a loan or line-of-credit
7. Join a startup incubator
8. Barter your services for their services
9. Joint venture with distributor or beneficiary
10. Commit to a major customer

Another way to outlast the Death Valley curve is to be financially ready. It doesn't mean you need all the money in the world to support it, but you should at least have an accountant ready to help you manage your finances. If you don't manage those finances properly it will come back and haunt your business. As you grow, your profits will increase to include the expensive fees in keeping up with the demand. For example, you might need to get a bigger facility for storing your products. Additionally, your wage bills will escalate to retain your employees, and most likely your paying more in taxes. This can be your subliminal message that transitions your business from a start-up to the growth phase. As a caution, if you don't have your expense under control it can go from start-up, to grow, and to failure.

In conclusion, the valley of death will test each entrepreneur his or her commitment, determination and wiliness to succeed. If you plan accordingly, you can survive the Death Valley curve by following the few steps above. Remember, if you manage your finances improperly you can lead your business right into the ground.

www.ingramcontent.com/pod-product-compliance
Lightning Source LLC
LaVergne TN
LVHW051021080826
845145LV00009B/2739